Radio Waves

Radio Waves

poems by
Genie Zeiger

Genie Zeiger

WHITE PINE PRESS / BUFFALO, NEW YORK

WHITE PINE PRESS
P.O. Box 236
Buffalo, New York 14201

With thanks to the following publications in which these poems first appeared:

The Prose Poem: "The Hole," "Woman on Chessboard" (under title of "The Piazza"), "The Wind." *Korone:* "On the Spine of My Life," "Make-up," "The Uses of Fiction," "My Mother Refuses to go to the Nursing Home." *The Georgia Review:* "The Queen of Sheba," "Radio Waves," "For My Mother at the End," "How Old Carl Broke His Back." *Key Satchel:* "Down and Up." *Earth's Daughters:* "Peculiar," "Falling." *This Wood Sang Out:* "The Visit." *Tar River Poetry:* "Annular Eclipse." *Proposing on the Brooklyn Bridge,* (anthology): "Marriage." *Bridges:* "To Go to Jerusalem," "Faith." *The Sun:* "Light, More Light."

With thanks to the women in my poetry classes for their companionship and deep inspiration. And abiding gratitude to Steve Corey for editorial expertise and care.

Cover painting: Bob Masla, "Going Home After the Storm." Used by permission of the artist.

Publication of this book was made possible, in part, with public funds from the New York State Council on the Arts, a State Agency.

First Edition.

10-digit ISBN: 1-893996-41-7
13-digit ISBN: 978183996410

Printed and bound in the United States of America.

Library of Congress Control Number: 2005929021

Contents

In memory of
Robyn Oughton
1947–2003

"Everything is in the hands of heaven,
except the fear of heaven."

—*The Babylonian Talmud*

Section 1

Faith

Not in what I know, this well-appointed house
with its shiny floors and strident houseplants,

but in a buried place, my life takes root, overflows.
There's no confusing desert with damp earth.

When I yearn and ache, lie awake between the off-white
cotton sheets afraid, listening to rain pummel the metal roof,

I remember a station, one where I once dreamed
I met my dead father, a depot in the middle of nowhere

that was safe, hard and true, and although I am deaf
in one ear and easily distracted, although my mind

with its unruly engine often races past that station,
I resemble those tumblers in a story I once read, Jews

packed into boxcars who disguised themselves as clowns sporting
piecemeal costumes hurriedly made en route

from bits of newspaper, foil from cigarette packs, shreds of prayer
shawls, strands of hair, a few clever folk who fooled

their captors with their antics—jumping, hooting,
wheeling down the wide aisles toward Auschwitz,

so convincing that, when the train stopped,
they leapt free from the boxcars.

This Body

This body is an animal rooting for bones,
a flower blossoming. This body is

brown from sun and lined by time;
it is at rest, learning how muscle,

sinew, blood and bone collude.
This body has fear, a retracted star for a heart

beating itself into a place so large
that death and love are the same there.

This body wants to dance, wail, embrace, run—
it is a blue doe about to leap over

an old stone wall, the hunter closing in,
but no matter, it will burst into light.

This body is a storehouses of treasures
in which preparations for a feast are underway—

silverware, goblets, golden plates, white
linen napkins folded again and again.

This body is small, crouching under the table;
it is large, looking down at the manufactured

world from a palace of cloud. This body is dry and wet,
vigor and fatigue, and I follow it, sniffing like a dog.

Willows

Each week work takes me past
the state troopers' building by the
highway and I want to blink away
the willows there because under them,
a long sigh ago, I used sex as a net
because I was afraid to lose a man,
a husband, because I believed he was
a cloak against the grim outside,
against all I could not know or own,
and so I stroked him, got him hard,
revived the old mechanism of our love-
making, then lay breathless beside him
looking up at those trees as he said,
"Man, that was weird," the fronds falling
long like my hair then, almost grazing my face.
Trembling legs, creased clothing, traffic hiss.

Place is memory, memory a wet truth:
for a decade I lived inside my idea
of that man, my hands damp from
clasping him until, under trees,
beside a busy highway, I used
my body as bait for the last time,
and he unhooked me for good.

Between Down and Up

When I looked up what I saw was
the underbelly of that small bird,

the nuthatch, gray, smooth and kindly.
A bird to fit in the palm, to carry

carefully as an egg, a seedling,
a lover's word. It was all cautionary

and holy. Pinions of its folded wings,
bones filled with air, incremental

feathers, and I wanted to love that exactly.
But when I looked down, what I saw was

the concave mirrored shape
of that bird's smooth, gray belly:

a grave expectation, a spot
in which to place a seed, an emptiness.

On the Spine of My Life

I sleep. I dream a host of butterflies
above my head, a baby without
a hat. I sleep. I wake. The sky is gray-
blue. Over my neighbor's house
an orange sun balloons up.
I think about her cancer, I don't know what kind.
I wash my face humming
a Hebrew prayer I learned in summer
camp when I was nine. I'm thinking
how enlightened I was for six days
after my son almost died
escaping the jungles of Peru.
Then an errand to *Rite-Aid*
for gauze pads was bliss.
Now I'm sipping tea at the big window—
strong black stuff with milk and honey—
biblical, the color of camels.
I read a psalm or a poem deep enough to haul
my mind above its habit
of listing what to do. I'm cooking
oatmeal, then I'm eating it, watching a grouse
in the poplar, finches at the feeder,
a rabbit chewing grass.
I think how animals have
direction and no words,
wonder what it feels like to live
in the wild, alert to nuance, afraid
of being bait. I open my journal,
mark the date: March 15, 2000.

I Can't Stop Staring

Officials Sanction Brief Visit Between North and South Koreans

In the news photograph, Park Kan Won
meets his mother, Miyong Og,
for the first time in fifty years:
his chin pressed against the end of her nose,
her mouth loosely open, the darkness between
parted lips down turned. His breath
on her face, his hand dwarfing her shoulder,
drawing her to him. Her dress
of pale aqua silk. His gray suit.
The long liver spot on her cheek, an island.
Her eyes squinting against the light of him.
His staring, eyebrows raised, as if into
all he never saw, the old wholeness at last.
Her hands, her eyes, the true
border between north and south.
Her hair neatly up in a bun,
the silk of his red tie on her chin.

Autumn

Yearning spreads its thin wings,
invisible bird with no visible tree,

unredeemed by the barking
of geese that falls from sky to

earth with its softening fruits and seeds.
The black clustered caps of yarrow,

curved wet limbs of maple,
the slow rains at night—

all is Exodus, things rushing
toward departure, and I too am

being stripped—oh darkness,
my larder, my receipt.

Lightning

is the body's alarm,
I know because God
once visited me
in a storm-filled drama
and almost killed me,
scared me so much
I married a sexy jailer,
a man I knew would one day
leave me, and so I sewed
myself to his insides
for a decade, struggled
like Jonah inside his fish,
confusing sweet love with
the reek of salty flesh until,
at last, he spit me onto dry land.

I am still being lured
by God into light.
I'm coming, I swear,
I cry from behind a damp
pink towel I pin to the line
to dry in summer sun
when the green arrowwood
raise their thousand hands,
birth their purple berries,
and sometimes the night sky,
that ancient Greek theater,
flashes its wake-up calls
and, on my knees
at the picture window,
eyes wide, I gasp

at the chorus of lightning bolts,
my cells shifting as I recall,
for a moment,
the bright trail home.

To Go to Jersusalem

after Adam Zagajewski

To go to Jerusalem, a city which may be nothing but pure idea.

To pack a book, a flowered dress, a scarf, a prayer, the memory of prayer.

To be a Jew leaving home willingly, with no one shouting.
To walk, not run.

To imagine the distant sounds of shoes on cobblestone as you leave alone in summer, walking past berry canes, ferns, grasses, sunflowers with seeded faces.

Or to depart in September, to fast the day before leaving, not in atonement but at the thought of Jerusalem,
something easily lost if more than pure belief.

To consider the Almighty, to not consider Him,
His rage and His demands.

To cut one's hair in a stylish fashion, to carefully fold one's clothing like money into small, neat piles. To use one's hands with care in packing, the way Aunt Esther did as she lifted a chicken bone, bit in slowly, then sucked the colored marrow.

To go to Jerusalem with ideas of sacrifice and barter, remembering thin refugee cousins from Europe with smiles and gold teeth.

To leave with a handkerchief in one's pocket, its edge embroidered a faded yellow.

To not think of exile, distance, language, war.

To consider Jerusalem as an old photo, holding it between
the thumb and forefinger, noticing a fat matron waving
a spoon, a patriarch in white standing next to a warning posted
in a drugstore window, *1943*: "Beware: The Enemy is Listening."

To return it to the Dutch biscuit box with Rembrandt's soldiers,
swords in hand, impressed upon its lid.

To hear at last what these soldiers say, what their wives and children
whisper under their breath, what God never said to any people.

To close the lid, in justification of history, motion, gravity. To smell
the metallic aftermath on your fingers.

To imagine sitting on a bench in Jerusalem feeling,
as when looking up at stars, as if you were a short candle burning.

Trying to Pray

New Year and this synagogue is a packed ship,
the air is water with thick language paddling up

through it towards the Holy One.
The old prayer book, its frayed black covers,

the Hebrew letters half familiar, crouching—
insects, refugees I try to hold between my hands.

Beside me, a mumbling old man who reminds me
of my grandfather, his prayer book open to the wrong page.

My shoulder vaguely touches his as my eyes drill
each page for something true, mine—

the story of a woman who crossed
her own Red Sea, birthed two children, lost

two parents and now stands on dry land, breathing hard.
In the intermittent silence between prayers,

the howl of an autistic boy strapped in a wheelchair.
I turn and, over a sea of faces, find his and

that of his bearded father mildly smiling beside him.
I turn back to my book, my lips forming ancient sounds

which ache to be true, but it's that wild boy's shrill cry
that is mine, rising now from God knows where.

From

I am from *come here,* and *forget it,*
from the sticky drip wax
of Sabbath candles lit by my mother,

from under my teacher's thumb,
from stalks of romaine lettuce leeching
in the sink, dust on the blinds and neighbors'

voices mixing with airplane roar, dish clatter,
Broadway and anon. I am from a death
camp liberated the day I was born, from

lead in a pencil, a fingertip lost to a knife,
the wheeze in my sister's chest,
the teeth wired inside my mouth, my smile.

I am from the blue of the caged parakeet's wing,
from Beth Jacob, the jammed orthodox *shul,*
from the Chevy assembly line, sharpened ice

skates, from my father's top drawer between
his ironed hankies and striped boxer shorts,
the belts, neatly rolled.

I am from the bad dream of bad waves,
Ivory soap, from mercury sliding
on the floor after the thermometer

broke, from my best friend's father dead
in the snow, matinees at the *Boulevard.*
I am from stickball, ballet, books, from

the Bulova watch factory across the highway,
from behind the closed Venetian blind, from Nestle's
and the subway, from I'm salt and I'm not sorry.

Belief, in August

I step gingerly
into the old pond,
mud rising at my feet,
clouds of it,
and I think of
Nagasaki, Dresden, Hiroshima
as I keep walking in,
leaving behind
whatever was—
the elegant, the terrible, the great.
The water, fed by
underground springs,
is cold, too cold, but
I keep entering
because I am
stupid with heat.
Slowly I step
naked, as if down
a watery aisle
to be married,
the tall maples lined up
on every side until,
waist deep,
I count aloud to ten
and then, plunging in
with a shriek, I'm wet
and received.

Toward Death

I tied red yarn to good
trees behind my first home
in the woods
so I could find my way
back, so I could hide from
the lightning that had once
almost killed me, red
threads to find my way
out from the tall towers
of Manhattan, the lesser
brick of Queens, from
my mother's fierce hand,
my father's crooked nose
to now where, beneath
a white pine, I hammer
words, footholds to carry me
down my own strange mountain.

What was I when I began?
An unsung psalm.
What will I be when I end?
A sprig of light, a tree,

I want to see and hold all
I stand to lose, all I crawl
or stride toward,
depending upon the day.

This morning, lying early in a field,
I squinted left and right into
the traffic of dew-ridden grass,
shopfuls of diamonds
reflecting a shining completion.
I know I am less than
light and water. More.
I know I must, in the end,
let go of everything,
let the sun, as it
ascends, dry me.

High Holidays

Again I don't know what do
on this high holiday, Yom Kippur,

which my blood sanctifies,
and my mind defies. So,

like the wandering Jews of old,
I go to yet another temple

to find God. I sit, stand
and listen, my finger moving

right to left under the dark,
curved letters, trying to match

sound with words. This poem,
that's what it's trying to do.

I'm tired of asking that old God
for forgiveness, let me forgive

Him and myself, let me
construe my own true liturgy.

But how do I take sounds
as old as Noah and build

a boat of them,
translate Moses' lisp,

or Sarah's joy when, at ninety,
she found herself, at last,

with Jacob's seed?
Let this poem be

like her child, a blood-stained
and eager form of praise.

Carrots

A bumper crop
all from one small
packet shipped
from Maine,
seeds thinner
than the period
after this sentence.
Now I hold foot-
long, tapered
carrots, like fingers,
some hairy, some
slick, like the "yad,"
used to demarcate
and bless the weekly
Torah reading.
I kneel, push
soil aside, pull
sideways so
as not to break them,
work the way
I do to find
happiness,
slantwise.

Arrangements

A branch of orange maple leaves in a blue vase
  "From Russia," my mother said.
    Without its handle, the terra cotta is visible

at the broken ends, same as always,
  but the leaves, newly placed there,
    turn their pallid undersides up,

like leaves drying everywhere. As I walk
  in the woods later with a friend, we can't hear
    each other because they blister so under our feet.

What makes me afraid?
  What is a greater thing than fear which,
    in the end, is thin?

When I fell hard in love, I got up. When my babies
  were ready, I pushed them out. When my mother
    was dying, I held her cool hand and sang.

But You, maker of seasons, filler of moon,
  move all things so quickly, so slowly
    sometimes I can't make you out at all.

Often a chair seems more serviceable,
  bread more generous,
    a rose fuller and more sweet.

You, Invisible One, the only
      way to see you
            is in each and every thing.

Traveling

Faith is a station
and my train starts,
then stalls on the tracks,
starts then stalls.
My angels are conductors
whose names I keep
forgetting, whose bodies
I keep bumping into.
Now I sit, fold my
inky wings and
press my nose against
the smudged window—
who cares what
I look like, the lines
creasing my cheeks,
the flesh cradling
my eyes, when I can
see trees, deep hills and
that imperishable city rising,
white spire and smoke,
in the blue distance.

In Spite of, Because

I will open the door
to the hidden place,
which is never a manger
but a harried nest
lined with blue feathers,
white...in spite of, because.
With my brown hair and eyes,
a loaf of rough bread and
sweet wine, I will enter
that dark, sit in the small temple
with its ten rays of light
remembering my generations,
the not so silent congregation,
the water of their prayer.
Around my shoulders
a shawl, a few threads unloosed—
wheat, my first child's hair.
I will try drinking God
from a small metal cup,
hold the old handle,
crooked like an arm,
bring its cool rim to my lips.
My chest bones will
rise and fall, rise and fall,
such a small ark for
my Jerusalem, Esther,
Job, my Red Sea.

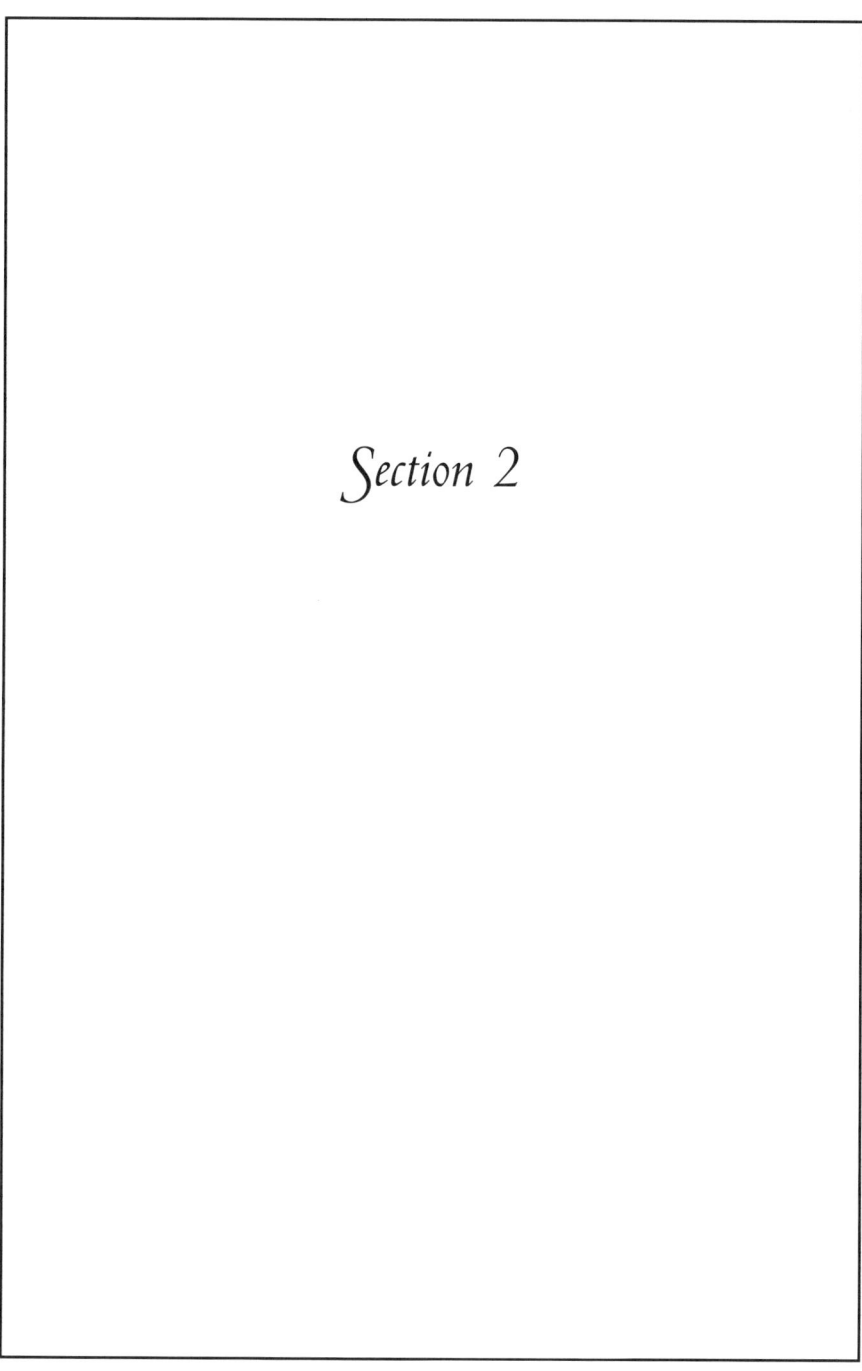

Section 2

Light, More Light

The storm would not abate
that night, the lightning

blinded me. He said
I arched off the bed a foot

or more screaming, he said he
thought I was struck and I was,

and when the dream sheets
of white light kept repeating,

I'd wake up trembling and
roll toward him. One night

after yet another bolt, I reached
for the bedside lamp and the bulb

lit and frizzled at my touch.
What did it mean?

He called me "witch" and I
married him, then lived for

a decade in the lesser light
of our fusion. Only it wasn't exactly

that, just need and lust scrawled tight.
But I was talking of light,

how it blinded and illuminated,
I was talking of visitation and power,

not the unbending lure of his eyes.

At the Renaissance Ball

I'm talking to Jackie, a woman about half my age,
when this guy from the *Society for Creative Anachronism*
steps on the open toe of my new shoe to get

to her, proving Gloria Steinem right:
Invisibility is what you get at fifty.
He expounds about her red hair's symbolism,

Celtic and otherwise, commends
her fair speckled skin. Beyond
his bald head, beaky nose and ratty

blue velvet jacket, the wall is lit
by a slide projector with the image of
Michelangelo's *Moses.* Two horns rise

from his head like small penises, his beard
is water, his eyes, which have beheld God,
as riveting as those of the barred owl

outside my kitchen window this morning,
its feathers riffling in a January wind
as a few jays shrieked past and

scattered their blue. For entertainment,
the medievalists joust, their sword tips covered
by tiny red plastic cups, and the Unitarian

minister, mildly soused, cries:
*Halt my good fellows! Surely we can
resolve this conflict peacefully!*

Above the fray, Moses's eyes again clamp mine.
Like the stars, they want silence.
The lights dim for dancing and I think:

there is no way to live without disappearing.
This morning the owl left that tree
the minute I turned my head,

wind swayed, chased the blue jays away
and God, back in the beginning,
left Moses with only tablets of stone.

Before We Were Born

I enter the shell of me, its pink
center in my mother's bottom drawer

where I am set between silk slips and hose.
Or else I'm in the matching highboy,

top drawer with my sister, pressed
between our father's ironed white handkerchiefs,

their rolled edges sewn tight,
like his mouth.

Beneath the mahogany headboard
of their double bed crowned by

a graven pineapple, night lays down
its heavy hoop, and they breathe deeply,

he toward the left wall, she toward the right.
A sparrow lights on the dark ribs of

the fire escape outside the window—
a cock of its head for the cries of the dead,

another for sky, and my sister and I
arrange ourselves in line to be born.

Two taps on clear glass, a gong, a sigh
as our parents turn, swim across

seas toward the shore of each other,
and the bed heaves and tilts.

How I Was Put to Bed

It was in the small apartment,
its long hall leading to a dark
metal door which opened to yet
another hallway, then a stairwell

down to the lit stage of a street—
wide noise, a day, the squint of it,
then darkness again, and
I am kissed and lowered onto

a bed with two pillows, boulders
covered by a forest green cotton spread.
Down I go into that field, that river
and green sky. The bed smells good

and quickly I inhale and fall
into sleep, into nothing, then my father,
hours later, carries me limp to
the gray velveteen couch so he and

my mother have somewhere to sleep.
I never woke under transport,
never knew how a day was manufactured—
my arms, legs, and eyes open to the living

room of yet another morning. So must it
have been with Eve waking in that
voluptuous garden, stunned, back
where she never remembered having started.

Happy

So long as you're happy,
my mother always said, *happy,* and I was,
even as I stared at our parakeet
dead on a white paper napkin in her lap,
its tropical body a green heavy
token below the black flag of Mom's hair.

I was happy because I 'd just danced
with Bobby Hall. I was muscle, pulse and
crimson, and I didn't need wings, new shoes,
not even the shiny button we all call moon
although, as I walked home that night,
I loved how it rose above the low brick buildings
and newly planted trees propped by sticks and ropes.

Later that night I woke, heart thumping,
sat up in bed and stared at the small distances
between the bars of light the streetlamp pressed
past the slatted blinds onto the ceiling.
With my tongue I teased the gaps
the orthodontist would soon close
with wires, and I knew right then,
for a moment, the actual distance
between a feeling and a word.

Peculiar

how my father always used that word *peculiar,*
as if it were a medicine, or a stone he kept

deep in his brown trouser pocket so he could
remove it at will, to stare at and admire,

like when we drove into the Catskills,
those great unconscious slopes...*peculiar,*

Dad would say, as if awe could be defeated
by three willed syllables. Or as we sat around

the kitchen table, our four bodies:
mother, father, sister, sister, shaping our own

Zeiger galaxy. And Mom would bring
out a new food, an artichoke let's say, and

Dad would look down on it, a serene and spiky
green steaming on the flowered plate, and then

as if to tame it, would announce *peculiar,* which is what
I still think, ten years later, of the fact that he is dead.

Radio Waves

Ray Charles and Betty Carter doing "Baby, It's Cold Outside,"
braiding a vocal rope that hauls me loose and

fast from my desk to the altar of two tall speakers,
stands and sways me in a square of sunlight

on a shiny maple floor, his voice gravel-smooth earth,
hers silk burgundy pain, the reservoir in my heart

breaking loose and wet into the sweet of his
pleading "stay baby," and her "I really must go,"

their voices fox-trotting, curved red and pressing me
toward desire, my right foot caught between a man and

a woman, the present and past, longing and its sad
aftermath—knowing in one lyric ripple that

if my father lived, he too would stop his all,
he too would sport a goofy grin

sitting in his old gray armchair as Ray keeps hammering
at Betty to stay, "your eyes are like starlight now," and

she juices out her reasons to go. And I see, as song
drives me past the usual exit, that my father is still

alive, that his unbroken line hauls me to this state,
love stronger than song, and "the baby it's cold don't go"

of wanting him is the coal in my old furnace,
my dark brilliant nugget of heat and of trouble.

Under Grandmother's Table

are the grownups' legs and feet, and
a curvy wooden board that holds the table up.

It has hard leaves and flowers, I feel
them against my back. It smells like polish

under here, and I don't know if it's from
the wood, or the shoes that come in pairs.

Father shoes are black or brown with
holes in the leather near the toes.

Mother shoes point in front like
starfish and have skinny long heels

that remind me of angel wands.
Under here is alone, even with my cousin because

we don't talk. I stare at Mom's nylons,
shiny and tight, and at her ankles full of little bones.

Dad's pants have a fold near the bottom, but
there's nothing in the crease.

While their legs are on vacation down here,
the grownups are talking, I can hear them

like airplane noise far off, but I don't understand
a word. I want to lick the nylons, the woolen

pants and leather shoes, to know how
it tastes, the world they make me live in every day.

The Visit

Sometimes the dead need to travel.
Unstoppable without weight,
they prefer the small hours
when streetlights are still on, though fading.
They like moving in packs,
sharing advice no one hears:
listen to the tongues of animals and plants,
remember everything with love.

Even with my heart's desire beside me
in bed, it's hard to sleep.
A coyote's cry recalls old appetites,
the barking of a neighbor's dog
makes me want to kill a dog. I sleep.
One of the dead, my father, angles
down inside a dream, the one in which
he waits in the ruined city
to which I always must return.
Again he's standing in the halo of a street lamp
burnished by ancient light, my own familiar,
the father I danced small and mute around,
evening after evening, all prayer stopped in my throat.

The dead don't traffic in language,
nor honor convention, but arrive in any old
disguise, such as this, the body of my father
without a body. He draws me to him with
a tenderness that's taught in heaven.
And if there's weeping or rejoicing, no one hears it,
only my tired, "Why now?" as I stand in his arms,
fists clenched, and again he disappears.

How I Found My Father

The hairs on my father's arms are soft and long,
Iike a cocker spaniel's. I want to pet them

while he holds the *Times,* a huge menu, in front of his face:
Fire on Park Avenue, Earthquake in Turkey.

His nose looks crazy in the bathroom mirror.
Why, Dad, why?

Because I broke it on the library steps in Brooklyn
when I was a kid. You were a kid? He nods

and the crazy mirror nose hops up and down.
Those library steps led like Jacob's ladder up

to God knows where, to my father,
an atheist, hidden behind his papers.

For years before he died with a tuna sandwich
in his hands, he repeated, like a mantra:

*Every man carries within him the world in which
he must live.* I thought I never entered his, filled

as it was with news, filled as my mine was with
wishy-washy reverie until, two weeks after his death,

he crashed into the room of my dreams, and
sixty years of stacked faded papers toppled

onto the green living room rug, and I saw his face.

Cardinal

I never noticed how the pale willow
opened its light green hands,

so many hands falling loosely
at the wrists, nor how the blood red

buds of maple swelled as one sky became
one hundred clouds. They turned to rain

that fell in oblong sheets and seemed
to close my doors and windows and let me

into some wet sleep. I never saw how
the sun could pray itself to setting,

or heard, as light turned violet, then
gold, the peepers' raucous chorus,

the woodcock's clumsy *bzeep.*
If only I had found the vernal pond,

one edge of it plump with gelatinous eggs,
inside them a thousand black commas,

the white dots of tadpoles already dead.
I wish I had learned better how to study

(to love) what is dying, my mother leaning
against the sink, her back a hook,

her mind a question, the black of her hair
gone white. Look, she says, slowly

nodding toward the yard. I never noticed
until then the actual red of a cardinal,

the one in her tall cedar, its brilliant
flag passing, a life in one flash.

Make-Up

The nurse at the home calls to say
my mother has painted her eyelids
with pink nail polish. *No more make-up*,
she concludes, *it's too dangerous.*
Add this to the list of never again.

I visit and her eyes are clear,
the white, the gentle brown.
She looks at me with her unspeakable
love, old as geography.
She doesn't remember this morning's
visit to the ER for her eyes,
asks me to look at a small box
of tissues, the word RUSSIA written
on the cardboard top in her shaky script.
It's very interesting, she adds.

I put the Marx brothers, *A Day at the Races*
in her VCR, then walk to the nurse's station
to retrieve her blue plastic case:
three lipsticks, purple eye shadow, two
eyebrow pencils, blush. I tell the nurse
about the movie, add, *Maybe she'll be
inspired to do even wackier things.*

I drive home, the box of make-up
in the passenger seat beside me:
an urn full of ashes, color without
purpose or home. And all I want is
to find a spot of ground to bury
it in, to say a sad and glamorous
prayer over it, crazy or not.

Florida

A small lake's watery face,
the lips of it drifting east.
A canopy of Spanish moss,
pale gray-green, falling from
trees, like a queen's tresses,
an earl's, the curls of a slave,
windswept. And sounds—
frog croak, man talk, dog talk,
engine groan, insect, bird whistle
and call, all buzz and chitter
and ask, ask, ask. But what for?
Even the dead are here, risen
in strident weeds, and my mother,
gone five years, now sits in the yellow
canvas chair beside me and suggests,
"Cheer up," my father, dead ten,
pipes in "Amen." They sniffed me out
in Orlando, not far from where
they retired, where I'd visit yearly
with the kids, was bored and baked
beside the perfect aqua pool before
we ate the early-bird specials.

How do I welcome them now
here beside live water that harbors
no rest and makes me sad?
Are you sure you want to stay? I ask.
They nod, start humming some show
tune I can't make out, then two-step
over the lake where Dad becomes
an orange butterfly flapping

deftly out of sight; Mom,
the small ache in my back.

Barred Owl

Its tail feathers shaking,
> long rags blown

in slanted wet snow,
> its eyes wheels of gold

as it sat in the oak
> the winter my mother died.

Storm after storm
> kept blowing in,

engines complained,
> white dreams exhaled,

and the owl arrived
> again and again

until its claws were her hands,
> its rags her pale dress,

and the earth, timid
> and closed by her death,

greened and let me
> love her again.

For My Mother at the End

If I give you something
to take with you, let it be

these words, their issue,
for with them I have held

much of what I love:
I have tamed the lion of my heart,

the sparrow of my fear.
I've made of them the city

we knew well: the soft eyes of cars
on the highway, Chopin through

the neighbor's door. And food
of our table, and desire never served.

There was a star you pointed towards
as you held me and said, *Star.*

You gave me words, now take
them back, swim your strong crawl

as you did when I watched you
small from shore. Take them:

lion, sparrow, city, car
door, food, mother, star.

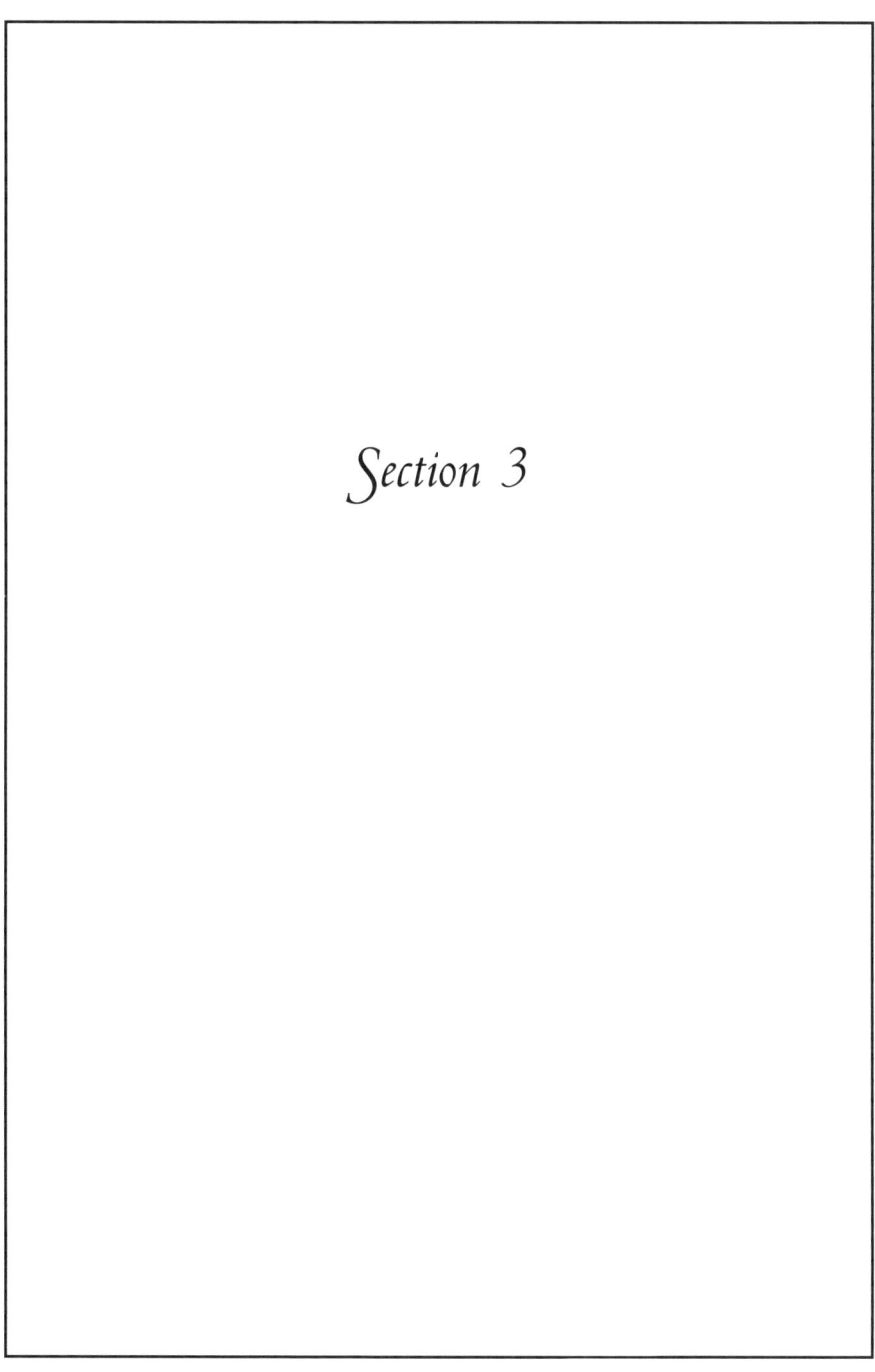

Section 3

The Queen of Sheba

I think of her as I run the single-edged razor
carefully up my right calf, then rinse the pepper white
foam and begin another pass. Twelve centuries ago
she grew rich controlling the major trade routes
in Arabia. Her pale camels, stilt-like, carried her spices,
their odors exaggerated in thin desert air.
In her palace, she was groomed by slaves:
hair brushed methodically, skin anointed with oils.
I move on to my left leg, thinking

that when I was a kid, a girl with ideas, like,
When I grow up I'm going to be a ballet dancer in France!
someone would always say,
Who do you think you are, the Queen of Sheba?
This was before I owned much except
my body, and all I could trade were baseball cards
with their faint sugary odor of gum.
I dry my legs with a blue hand towel,
then spread it out on a rack to dry.

King Solomon, renowned for wisdom, found
the true mother when he held a baby up in the air
and threatened to slice it in half.
In *The Song of Songs* he declared:
Beloved, Your hair is like a flock of goats...
Sheba, intrigued, paid him a spicy visit,
showered him with gifts. Rumors flew of
the impending wedding of wisdom, wealth, and beauty.
Once I knew I had it all. My long hair blown

by the wind, I walked between my fiance and
his friend, an actor, in the Central Park Zoo, down
the paved paths between the monkeys and giraffes.
Little kids scooting past, popcorn flying
from red and white boxes, trees leafing out.
We made a caravan, me in my suede miniskirt
wedged between the men, behind us my parents.
The Red Sea had parted and I was very tall.

Rumor had it that Sheba, though lovely, had
the legs of a donkey. Solomon devised a plan.
In front of his throne he constructed a platform of glass
shining like water: Sheba approached,
raised the hem of her skirt not to wet it, and
at last he saw those infamous legs:
shapely, yes—and yes, they were hairy.

When we reached the crossroads in the park, my mother
motioned to me, and I walked quickly toward her.
Turning away from my father, she said fiercely,
*You're jiggling, it's disgusting, where's your girdle,
your bra?* I looked at her and sighed.
Is this my true mother, the one who would have me?

Solomon continued to assess his situation,
had depilatories concocted by magicians,
persuaded Sheba to use them and then become
his wife. She agreed, but there was a price, she was Sheba:
Solomon would give half his land, his entire heart.
Stars shot across the skies on their wedding night,
the planet tilted, and Haile Selassie, future Emperor of Ethiopia,
was conceived. Outside the door, servants eavesdropped,

silks draped on their arms, cool pale
drinks sweating in clear glasses on trays.
We drove home from the zoo in my parents' Chevy,
an arid silence, my father's onyx ring clicking on
the steering wheel. I sat alone in back, staring
at featureless rows of pale houses lining the parkway,
an occasional awkward body of water reflecting dull sky.
I stared at the black flag of my mother's thick hair, brushed
the short grain of my skirt down over my thighs,
wondered, *Who in the world did she think she was?*

Twenty Years Since the Wedding, Ten Since the Divorce

Water under the bridge,
those years we sped home
then rubbed our bodies together,

as if friction might inspire
a grand hotel with an elegant feathered
bed in which we'd never die.

In the old photo, the two
of us on the swing in our yard,
my long hair parted down

the middle, a smile sizeable enough
to hold happiness. Your head poised above
mine, Jesus hair, honey-eyed,

our four hands clasping
the thick ropes. Today I read Keats
to Earl who is dying of heart

failure, and when the nightingale arrived,
all I heard was Earl's labored breath,
which made the red flannel of his shirt

visibly fall and rise. Driving home,
the same machinery that keeps
Earl's heart pumping, my dreams receding,

brought you, after years, into view—
frizzed hair, full lower lip, your pale profile
in a red pick-up, and my heart raced

as I gripped the wheel hard, remembering
the old aqua three-quarter ton
we bumped along in, thigh to thigh,

past fields of stone, tobacco, birds,
corn, years when we couldn't bear
even an inch of space between us.

Falling

It began with the sun
worship, my old yoga routine—
I raised my arms above my head
in salute, then stretched forward,
the world spun, and I fell dizzy with it
onto the blue-green ocean, I mean carpet.
Every time I turned my head,
it revolved, the world I could see.
And so I lay still for hours,
as if in the bottom of a moored canoe,
and let the virus pass and it did.
Next day I decided to go to a dance class,
and in the dusk of downtown, my car
glanced the body of a man in a long black
coat crossing at the far end of the pedestrian lane.
He fell sideways, ungracefully,
(I can still see him), then got up very slowly,
wiping his sleeves. A crowd gathered as
someone led him by the arm, like a child,
to a pink chair in the brightly lit Asian
nail salon nearby as I pulled to the curb,
left the car running, ran and kneeled
beside him, crying, "Are you okay?"
"I'm fine," he said.
His glasses sat on his face like furniture.
An ambulance came, then the police,
Officer Williams who said, "It's fifty/fifty,
maybe fifty-one/forty-nine,
only a warning," and I sat
in my car for twenty minutes
as blue lights flashed behind me and

the cop did the copious paperwork.
Back home that night I picked at supper
and worried the evening along
until the man I sort of hit called to say,
"I'm fine, I was worried about you,
I want you to sleep tonight." And sleep
did come, slowly, the way a poem comes,
the trees growing white and lacy because
now it was snow, lovely and gracious,
that was falling.

Borders

When I threw a stick into the middle
of a small vernal pool, we watched
ripples ride, waves propagate to the edges,

and then a floating oval
reflecting floating sky.
It was oddly erotic because

we'd made love that morning
and the way our edges drifted, our
separation stretched to broken,

made me cry, as I had the night before,
when I'd heard how Billie Holliday
and Artie Shaw's all-white band

had to pay double to eat
in the kitchen of a restaurant in Georgia
because of Billie's skin. After the water

settled to stillness, we climbed to
High Ledges, watched the silver river
unwind to the west, a hawk tilt toward

its invisible prey in the hills. Billie
needed the bathroom, and when she
asked the hostess, her arms clasping

a wall of menus to her ample chest, where
it was, the woman snapped, "No toilets for you
Coloreds." The trees below us were budded,

suggestive of red, of spring, of pale green
doors about to open. "Well, now just what
do you suggest I do?" Billie asked the woman,

"I'm 'bout to burst." As the woman shrugged,
Billie lifted the hem of her off-white dress and let
loose, really let loose. What else was there to do?

When the Darkness is Deep

When the darkness is deep, figures
begin to appear at the place where
you and sky collide. First they
resemble the ones you drew as a kid.
Then, like your body, they blossom,
fill the space between you and mystery.

When the deep is dark, larger figures
appear, yours and not yours, now
and much later in the place without clocks.
But now is, as when on the phone
you said, *Now I feel good.*

So when darkness takes you down
with her vast tender hands, trust in the earth
of her making, in the yeast of your fear,
the water of your courage, the heat
of your good heart. For you will rise up

over and over after being pressed lovingly
down just the right number of times
to be covered, baked in the bowl of her hands
until you become the finest bread
which family, friends, neighbors,
even strangers in shops will see, taste and
wonder: *What is the recipe for that?*
How can I become that?

—for Mary Ann Baker

Mine

We all have eyes for our own dark angel.
—Rimbaud

There she is, up on the screen,
eyes the color of excrement and
earth. Nothing is X-rated
in my dark angel's *Paramount.*
She's the star that weasels me
down into suffering and complaint
because she loves what I do not:
the persistent list of no good's,
the low cost of pain.
Nose buried in my neck, breath
on my skin, she whispers sweet
nothings, procures strands
of my hair, my weird dreams
of killing chickens. She takes
more of me, then more,
my personal trainer
ripping me off,
charging me blind.
Her deer eat my flowers.
Her birds, barely feathered,
croak wild at dawn.
Try closing the window,
try locking the gate.

The Uses of Fiction

Wolf-man, sneak-man Ned with those
lines of his leading me into
the stacks where he shoved me
against the S-Z novels,
Saroyan, Thackery, Yarborough,
him on me with whispers and
hands, his breathing
as the darkness outside
the Victorian library filled
with history, adventure, romance,
and the Susquehanna across the
street kept moving south, its riverbeds,
his hands pressing me, his
whisper of *It's okay,*
relax, the spines of the
books stuck in my back
and me without a word, without
one of the characters in the hundreds
of books I'd read by then, nothing
intervening as Ned was
on me, my back pressed
hard against book
after beautiful book.

Come Back

here among those who often take
it all for granted—morning
calls of kids in the long hallway, the clock's
steady drip, smell of pancakes cooking
on the iron griddle, and Thanksgiving
leftovers plastic-wrapped in the fridge.

Yesterday, dopey from morphine, your
voice piecemeal on the phone from
the hospital telling me the doctor
said, at best a year or two.
"I can't go there," you cried,
"I want four score" and I answered,
maybe too quickly to save us,
"Don't worry, we'll be old ladies together."

Dearest friend, I'll use whatever words
I can unearth to build a path of stone or air
for you from now to when we'll look back
and say, "God, what a nightmare," and
I'll repeat the story of how, after
you called with your awful news,
I saw a hawk try to snag a titmouse
at the feeder, miss, then glide low
over my head into the trees,
of how the titmouse, its crest flattened in fear,
chirped wildly in the apple tree nearby,
then quieted down, and came back to feed.

—For Robyn Oughton

When I Kissed Bill,

the old stones in our yard woke up and
got nosy, the trees creaked, stretched their limbs.

Charles and Jimmy, David and all
my old lovers sighed, then stared

out the windows of their offices and studios.
Bob, the sculptor, arrested his chisel mid-air,

an inch from the breast of the sandstone
woman he was finishing. I kissed Bill

and my goddaughter Liza was born,
up she grew fast as the pile of candies

in my trick or treat bag in New York,
as the waves offshore in Fort Lauderdale

where, as we swam in them, we saw
a rainbow above the Ramada, but I knew

it was really my mother whom we'd buried
that morning five miles away.

I kissed Bill and a galaxy went blind, the path
to the clear lake grew clear, the words of a great book

lined up to be read. It was fall, and
the goldenrod opened gold for the bees.

Love,

when you touch me, the animals
in the ark remember they are
paired. In the tall mahogany
bureau drawer in New York,
my father's tidy pile of white
handkerchiefs tilts to the right.
A solitary fox in the woods beyond
our yard halts, raises a sleek head and listens.

When you kiss me, the metal
in an auto parts factory in Detroit
glows molten as it is bent
into usable shape—a fender, a hood.
The feathery dark shaft of a marigold
seed dreams its orange and crimson.

When you enter me, you open all my doors—
the one to the full, locked
closet, the one I closed bereft
in the bad woods of bad years,
the bee's narrow entrance to her hive
where waxy combs drip with sweetness.

Sunday Morning

Dedicated to Fred Rogers

So Bill says, he says to me,
I dreamed Frankenstein wanted to have sex with me,
and I ask, benignly sliding toward him in bed,
So what did you do?
and he says, looking at the ceiling,
I talked him out of it.
And because it's Sunday morning
and March and sleeting and Mr. Rogers
died only a few days ago, I sing
what Mr. Rogers always sang to make
little girls feel complete without penises,
although he never mentioned them:
"Some are fancy on the inside,
some are fancy on the outside,
everybody's fancy, everybody's fine,
your body's fancy and so is mine," and I wonder,
for a second, about Frankenstein's privates
as Bill says, he says to me, F*unny,*
I never use that word.
What word? I ask.
Fancy, he says, and I tell him that
this guy on the plane from Miami,
(I'd recently flown home from Miami),
he says to me, *splendid* this and
splendid that, and Bill, rolling over
and pecking at my cheek says,
I don't say splendid either and
then we get up to a lackadaisical
Sunday in the neighborhood,
except for the sighting of a gray squirrel

executing acrobatic feats in an assault on
our bird feeder that would put
Houdini to shame and I say to Bill,
That guy reminds me of a furry,
obese insect and he says, *Maybe*
a worm and what we do is we bang
on the big picture window while
simultaneously yelling in a very un-
Mr. Rogers like manner until said
squirrel takes off with its pathetically
nervous tail into the un-thoughtful
falling of cold hard things, I mean
sleet, and I say to Bill, *I guess*
this is a good day to do my taxes,
and Bill, he says nothing but nods
his pale face with its high Periclean forehead,
and I go and clear my desk of all the books and
papers and poems that make for my
splendid life and reach for awful
piles of cancelled checks, receipts,
W-2s, 1099s, wishing I were the grouse
or the goldfinch I see in my yard
from my vantage point at the desk,
thinking anything would be more fun,
but without the feathers, I say to myself,
I'd be a goner and my kids and friends
would wail, not to mention Bill,
who is moving chairs and the table
from the shiny wooden
floor so he can mop it.

Marriage

Sometimes I'm married to a house.
Floorboards caress the balls of my feet,

the walls inquire how I am, ivy twines
up the bathroom wall in my name.

Sometimes our land, June-full of flowers, birds,
and trees is my ceiling, the rain my floor.

I walk on air or water, depending upon the light
or my ideas. I lose track of my husband: he could be

Brando, Jehovah, or my mother Ruth, depending
upon the day or my need. I remember my parents

foxtrotting to Sinatra across the small Oriental rug,
smiles on their lips, as I sat watching

from the green couch swinging my legs,
my mouth open as our parakeet

held to her perch looking bored.
Sometimes I'm married to the birds:

a phoebe, long-tailed and plain,
keeps trying to build its nest on a ledge

too small; each morning I sweep up
strewn grasses and straw, the waste of

feathers and time. A redthroat visits the feeder,
opens her attenuated beak, dips into the pink

sugar water my husband provides. Sometimes it's him
I'm watching, the river of his back, the hay-colored

crest of his head, his left hand holding
a cup under the shiny faucet,

which is long and bent, like a spent sunflower,
a hook, a dream.

After Surgery in Spring

I.

The dead say, "Live, you lucky one, look,"
and yes, I love the way the clouds rise,
haystacks in a sky blue sky,
how three plump cucumbers
burgeon under the overgrown weeds,
how my scar slowly turns from red
to white, a bright ladder to my heart.
I love my children's bodies, the eyes
of friends, my husband's sensible
grip in this time of darkness and green.
And though praise is in the cupboard,
in the wren's song, in the bee
balm of another day, I am set like clay
in some corridor, troubled by fear of what cut
me open and closed me up

2.

Maple buds redder,
bird rhetoric louder,
the lilac with its pale crown, everything
leaning toward infinity
like the figure 8's I made over and
over on ice as a child, my thin arms
extended, skates flashing as
I leaned into the curve.
Now I sit day after day and
stare into sky striated by clouds,
backdrop for the sun-stunned trees.

Now that I know there is no cancer,
what is wanted of me?

Last night, 2 A.M., as I turned over
in bed in pain, my father entered
the room—the blond hairs on his arms,
the slope of his forehead, his mute love—
I asked, "What must I do now?"
and he said, "Turn the light on,"
which is what we said in New York
to mean boil the water, heat the potatoes.
A decade dead, in the dead of night, he repeated,
"Turn the light on" and I knew
he meant not the stove, not the domed
ceiling fixture nor the bed-side lamp,
but the light.

The Wind

Down the early roads, the wind scatters dry
leaves in packs; they remind me of bugs or mice racing
spuriously anywhere—over the metal sap buckets that
have blown off the maples, over the edge of
the stubbled cornfield.

Something is wrong; it requires a rearrangement
of shape, of intent, as when Laurie was dying. She asked,
Remember me in the wind, and I do: her sparest of frames,
her eyes burning above the bones.

The wind has knocked out power and phone service.
I can only talk to myself now—what has happened to this world?
I look out the big window and think:
This is the silence you have held out for.

What the Poem Wants

Not the tooth, but the jawbone
Not the recipe, but the stew simmered all afternoon
Not the day's news, but the street
       on which it happened, the woman
       leaning out the window to see
Not those fingers, but your touch
Not the blatant day at noon, but
       the dream inside it
Not the I.V. dripping, but the healing
Not brakes or cables, but the Chevy's metal
Not Confucius, but Job in his ashes, grieving
Not the map, but the territory, green, wet and brazen
Not a stroll meanwhile, but a walk now
       up the hard incline to the chimney,
       all that's left of the house
Not the house, but the architect's first conception of it,
       the movement of pen to paper,
       the straight line placed there
Not the glossy black and white, but my mother herself
Not the sea, but the fish hoisted out of its waves
Not the siren, but the building up in flames

Some Views of the Dark

—for Greg Gillespie

I didn't know what a frame could hold until
I saw the indigo bunting's blue blaze outside
my window the day I learned Greg hanged himself.

I knew I loved his painting, "Studio Corner":
a white table set with a nest-like bowl,
a butternut squash, one clean hammer, and under

the table a self-portrait in which he's young, bearded, and
looks at me over his left shoulder. I imagined his right hand
placing a single-hair paintbrush down on that table,

then picking up the rope. Then I watched the bunting
take off toward the birdhouse set among
the budded saplings with their markets of lime-

colored leaves near the slow river of our road,
its crested center and wide curves high
on our hill above all the inexplicable traffic.

Walking outside, I found a few dun-colored stalks,
grasses the shade of my husband's hair, my sister's skin,
then went inside to study Greg's paintings again

as if I'd find solace or answer in one burial place
in which green tapered grasses splay star-like
in five directions beside a wooden urn, a fallen log,

and a darkness I couldn't stop staring into
that reminded me of my mother long at her dying,
telling each person who arrived at her bed

with a cup, a diaper, a pill, how beautiful they were.
Her face was a cloud, her hands thin branches.
I always knew I loved her, Ruth was her name,

but I didn't know I could love darkness,
how it takes in all things, yet never fattens.

Smelling the Buddha

Because the fox circled our house
under a big-faced moon, then rubbed

its hide against the statue, we discussed
omen, fact, and blessing. Because the guidebook

said, "Red foxes spray when mating
in January, check for a skunk-like odor."

Because the mind can rub against anything,
and the stars just hang out above it all

until we are drawn into sleep.
Next day I awoke, the engine of my body cool,

dressed and crossed the icy yard, the garden
of woebegon sunflowers, heads bent

like old-fashioned streetlamps, the Buddha
sitting small in the center facing west.

Dark small weeds made an aura around
his famous lap and a bit of green drooped

beside his right knee. I bent, then sniffed his head,
and the dead garden made me glad. Because I went

to town that day, I saw a man in a leather jacket opened
to the waist, his chest bare. Beside him, a woman

with a black eye. What I smelled was trouble.
Because god is a fox that circles and breathes me

to attention, because what lives at the center
is always surprise, on one day

I saw a Buddha in the dead garden
and a beaten woman on a bad man's arm.

The Whores of Tuscany

One sits, black-skinned and thin, on an overturned
plastic bucket, her back to oncoming traffic,
her baseball cap backwards in the direction

of nearby San Marco where, in fresco,
fine gold encircles Magdalene's head and
her robe sweeps pink and sheer below her

as she kneels beside the right hand of Christ.
At the next rest area, another, in fishnet
stockings, straddles three feet of pavement,

meeting the Autostrada head on.
Under her red leather very
miniskirt, her legs seem

done in stone, gorgeous slopes
of chiseled flesh both hard and soft at once.
A crown of braids above a face

to launch a missile or two,
and no veils, nothing
to conceal her in the tireless market

of the open air. Sometimes driving
past her station when she's gone, I picture
her in a field of scarlet poppies crushed

under some panting Signor while his
Alfa Romeo idles nearby. Or in the back
of the white Microbus, parked in the turnoff,

where the *Madam* always sits,
her plate of a face fixed behind
the wheel always staring, as I do,

at these lush green hills,
the pearled distances that
enclose us all in their folds.

Over the Hill

I'm over the hill and no one's interested
in watching how fast I'm going.

They're at the movies, at work, or
on some island soaking up sun, fastened

like starfish to hot sand. They're grooming
and fretting over themselves and each other,

especially if they're the 51% with softer,
rounded edges which, like the curve of the world,

they ache to preserve. And if their bodies
are more like the straight line I'm writing,

they're men climbing mountains, corporations,
ladders. They can't help it, they want to get

somewhere. But me, I've got a vowel stuck,
like a chicken bone, in my throat as I try to

say prayers I learned as a child so God will
bless and pity me—me with my Torah, my river,

my hills of questions, my six million, and
two dead parents in my arms.

How is it that I can carry so much,
yet keep falling at the same time?

How Old Carl Broke His Back

It was in the living room, on the gold
rug between the TV anchorman,
with his usual terrible news, and
a shelf with color photos
of the kids smiling hard.
He was trying to lift the moon-
faced Elaine, his wife of fifty-three
years, large and half blind, after she fell.
Carl kept trying to pull her
up, to lift all the cherished things—
butterfly, fox, hummingbird, jay,
a truckload of daffodils he planted
ages ago so they would rise and
orate in their yard every May.
He grew confused.
Was he a flower, a man, or a hawk
dipping, trying to hoist
her up as she kept repeating, *Stop,
call 911, you'll hurt yourself.* But
he couldn't stop tending the monarchs
he built small milkweed homes for,
the indigo bunting he lured
to the feeders in June, the rocks he
cradled, wrapped in tissue paper and
set neatly in stacks, the dahlia
bulbs heaped brown and dry
in tall barrels—her voice, her body,
every flower, each vine
he tied up with wire and with twine,
every finch, weed, and stone screaming,
Please, you'll kill yourself, stop.

Omens

Although I share a queen-size with my husband,
at night before sleep I play solitaire and

sometimes a reckless card will stray to the floor.
I consult it in the morning, make

meaning feasible: ace of hearts=unadulterated love;
three of spades=buried grief.

The lukewarm water in the blue glass
beside me on the night table is oblivious,

as is the bedroom rug with its Aztec
design, claw-like creatures repeating

themselves as if pattern implies certainty.
But it does not—this summer

a screen door, properly hung,
slammed into my ankle, which required

five stitches. The doctor used black thread.
As it healed, I thought of Achilles, not Judas.

Today as late morning light
glazed the oak table, I burned my toast, but

because bread is innocent,
I thought of the dead, not the hungry.

Barred Owl, Again

November woods are
stick-like, slick

wet brown leaves
that grew from green

and fell. Then a glimpse
of the owl gliding over my head

to settle on a dead tree twenty
feet from me. Black, its eyes

feather-circled pools.
We stared at each other hard

as I cried for the death of a friend
I couldn't stand to lose.

The bird spelled me in the dark
of the dark of her eyes, took in

my moans, snuffling,
body shakes—the panoply

of human grief. Now and then
she swiveled her head,

then stared
back at me again—

a mother, benign...
a friend, a lover, true...

a predator, vigilant,
as if grief were her food.

The Hole

Today I ironed a woolen shawl, which a woman in Calcutta spent six months embroidering. She sold it for a song because the buyer, my ex-husband, found three moth holes at one end. I'd never bargain with that woman, I'd never offer her fewer rupees because of a few small holes.

The hole in the shawl is the hole in the screen that lets the flies in, is the hole in the world through which people come and go, is the "luch in kup" my father ascribed to the truly dumb. The rabbit scurries into it, the snake; it is the space between the rocks through which the sheep flee, through which the world enters, shyly at first, then brazenly.

The hole is the proverbial eye of the needle, the gap between teeth, the rip through which the dead return with their old coats and hats, with the sound of feet stamping to loosen the dust.

Mend it, fill it, glut it, wet it, stitch it, paste it, stuff it with vowels, consonants, entire dictionaries, and nothing works. What can you do? There's the hole. How can you fit into that tiny space gracefully, then live in it with so little room?

On Seeing "King Lear"

The fool crouches and clings to the mad
King's leg, laughs and weeps, common and noble,

with his "little tiny wit." I'd love to touch his cap
full of wildly colored feathers, twigs, things.

I want to leap on stage, give Goneril a shove and
grab sexy Edmund, let his blood, muscle, and skin

overtake my own. I want to be the blue of Cordelia's eyes,
her tears when her father knows not who she is; when he does.

I want to be Lear's rage, the storm, thunder and
virtual rain falling down that mesh curtain high

above the plain wooden stage. I want to be
clamor, kneel, parry and moan. I do not want to be

that stuffed, upside down goat, its four hooves tethered
to a long stick, nor any of the four dead on stage at the end of Act V.

I want to be grief so clean, passion so confusedly pure,
but most of all I want to be these words issued

from bodies that breathe and sweat and stride and bleed
until the lights go out. And I want to be life so quickly resurrected

as the actors return amid *Bravos* and wild clapping,
each a body that bows and receives easily among others of its kind.

And I want to be death when, like Lear, I am
fourscore or more, and the silence in the end, when

the lights come back on and we sit stunned, that too is what I want,
stillness punctuated only by the fool's song, which I can't get

out of my head, "Hey, ho, the wind and the rain," as I stare
at the stage, bare but for a stray button and one worn

red feather and his song repeating once more and again:
"Though the rain...the rain it raineth every day."

Woman on a Chessboard

after a photo by Edward Judice

The ground below me has grown hard and meticulous, a field of angles, a patchwork of black and white, clearly delineated, but nothing pure about it, the dark full of lesser dark, the white riddled by the less than white. Standing here, I am Electra after she finally finished wailing over her brother, I am a mother having waved a last handkerchief to her oldest child.

My shadow, to my right, lowers my hopes, then raises them, lays them beside me with something of myself inside, small now, a girl. It's a matter of sun, desire, astronomy, a little wind, how my shoes fit, what I've had or not had for breakfast, dreamed in the wee hours as the sun begins to stagger to its feet.

The hand of God is gnarled, bony and veined, like good marble. I used to believe that hand raised above me, giving directions—checkmate, take the pawn, pass. It was all in black and red, or black and white, the players embellished and implacable. There were directions in writing, rules. But so much time has passed since I first read them that I could be one of those headless Greek statues, all stone and hard garment, but the cool air is so pleasing now, here under my arms, and—Ah—my skirt has just blown its silk against my knees.

About the Author

Genie Zeiger lives in Shelburne, Massachusetts, where she has led creative writing workshops and poetry classes for more than a decade. The winner of a Massachusetts Cultural Council award for poetry, she has received numerous grants to lead writing workshops at senior centers, public schools and for Hospice. As a trained Hospice volunteer, she has worked with patients, caregivers and with the bereaved. A collection of writings by the members of one of her bereavement groups, *Oh, My Ashen Friend*, was published in 1996. She leads workshops to explore Jewish identity through writing at various synagogues in the northeast including Keene, N.H., Greenfield, MA and Northampton, MA.

Her first collection of poetry, *Sudden Dancing*, was published by Amherst Writers and Artists Press in 1988; her second, *Leaving Egypt*, was published by White Pine Press in 1995. Her first memoir, *How I Find Her: A Mother's Dying and a Daughter's Life*, was published by Sherman Asher Publishing in 2001, with a German edition by Kinder Verlag. Her second memoir, *Atta Girl!*, was published by Sherman Asher in 2005. Ms. Zeiger serves as poetry editor for the Massachusetts Audubon Society's magazine, *Sanctuary*. She has been a regular commentator on WFCR, public radio in Amherst, and on WAMC in Albany, and has given public readings of her work at bookstores, synagogues, libraries, schools and hospitals. Her poems, stories and essays have appeared in *The New York Times Book Review*, *The Massachusetts Review*, *The Georgia Review*, *Tikkun*, and *The Sun*, in which she has published over a dozen essays and interviews. Her work has been nominated twice for the Pushcart Prize. A former psychotherapist and crisis clinician at a mental health center, she has an M.Ed. in Counseling Education from the University of Massachusetts and an MFA in writing from Vermont College.